Living Long and Loving It!

Scripture Text:
All Scripture quotations in this publication are from the Holy Bible, New International Version.
Copyright© 1973, 1978, 1984, International Bible Society.

Additional Text:
Stephen Lang and Adelaide Teninga
© 1987 The Bible League
South Holland, IL. U.S.A.

Photographs:
cover--Comstock
pp. 16, 20, 32--H. Armstrong Roberts
pp. 2, 6--Jim Whitmer
pp. 5, 19, 24, 37, 38--Camerique

Published by
THE BIBLE LEAGUE

South Holland, Illinois 60473, U.S.A.
Weston, Ontario, Canada M9N 3N3
Penrith, N.S.W. 2750, Australia
Auckland 8, New Zealand

Printed in U.S.A.   A100-0035

This is what the LORD says . . .
"Listen to me, . . .
>*you whom I have upheld since*
>>*you were conceived,*
>>*and have carried*
>>>*since your birth.*
>*Even to your old age*
>>*and gray hairs*
>*I am he,*
>*I am he who will*
>>*sustain you.*
>*I have made you*
>>*and I will carry you;*
>*I will sustain you*
>>*and I will rescue you."*
>>>*—Isaiah 45:18; 46:3,4*

THE BEST FOR LAST

GO FOR THE GOLD!

That's *not* a campaign slogan—
   rather, it's a motto
      to encourage you
   to look forward to
      those "sunset" years
      when you can enjoy
   the best times of your life—
   golden hours . . . days . . . years!

The *best* at last!

If you have just "retired,"
   a fifth of your life
      may still be before you!

Or, you may be among
   the half of those
      over 85 years
   who claim no physical disability.

Then again, you may be part of
   that rapidly increasing number
   of centenarians
   who, each week,
      reach 100 years of age!

So, what will your life be like?
What are you going to do
   with those precious,
      fleeting moments each day
   in those "sunset" years
      that can be quite beautiful? . . .
   The last, but in some ways,
      the best!

*They [the righteous]
    will still bear fruit
        in old age,
they will stay fresh and green,
    proclaiming,
        "The L<small>ORD</small> is upright;
        he is my Rock,
        and there is no wickedness
            in him."
            —Psalm 92:14,15*

*Teach us [O Lord]
    to number our days aright,
    that we may gain
        a heart of wisdom.
Satisfy us in the morning
    with your unfailing love,
    that we may sing for joy
        and be glad all our days.
            —Psalm 90:12,14*

*Gray hair
 is a crown of splendor;
it is attained
 by a righteous life.
  —Proverbs 16:31*

*Is not wisdom found
  among the aged?
Does not long life
  bring understanding?*
  —Job 12:12

LIFE

LIFE . . . that mysterious vital force
   passed down through
       countless generations
   from the Source of Life Himself—
       God, the Creator!
   What a treasured gift!
   You did nothing to obtain it,
       but it is yours.
   And how you cherish it!
   How you protect it
       and try to prolong it!

But, "Why was I born?"
   "What is the purpose of my life?"
Surely you have asked yourself
   those perplexing questions.

Scientists have no answer
   because they deal only with
       the physical aspect of life,
   and you are more than
       just a *physical* human being.

The Creator gave you a soul—or spirit—
   for he created you "in his image"—
   different from all other forms of life.

Your spirit is clothed in your
   wondrously designed physical body.

Your body eventually dies,
   but your soul lives on—eternally!

Believe it . . . there *is* a reason
   for your existence.
       God makes no mistakes!

*The L*ORD *God formed man*
from the dust of the ground
and breathed into his nostrils
the breath of life,
and man became a living being.
—Genesis 2:7

So God created man
in his own image,
in the image of God
he created him.
—Genesis 1:27

It is the spirit in a man,
the breath of the Almighty,
that gives him understanding.
—Job 32:8

The dust returns
to the ground it came from,
and the spirit returns
to God who gave it.
—Ecclesiastes 12:7

A PLAN FOR YOUR LIFE

Perhaps you did not know
    that the Creator has a plan
        for *your* life!

"How can *I* know that plan?" you ask.

There is but one true source
    of information about life—
        how to live it successfully
        so that you may experience
            peace, joy, and happiness . . .
Those things everyone is searching for!

The Holy Bible is God's guidebook
    for living your life
        here on earth.

The truths found in the Scriptures
    increase your wisdom.
Those truths, if applied,
    are life-changing.
That divine revelation
    provides true understanding—
    changes your way of thinking
        in ways that are practical.

As you absorb those truths,
    you grow in ways
        you never thought possible.
And you discover
    what God had in mind
        for YOU!

Your understanding of that plan
    could bring
    a new zest for living.

*The word of the L*ORD *to Jeremiah:*
> *"Before I formed you in the womb*
> > *I knew you,*
> *before you were born*
> > *I set you apart;*
> *I appointed you as a prophet*
> > *to the nations."*
> > > *—Jeremiah 1:5*

A Psalm of David:
> *O L*ORD*, you have searched me*
> > *and you know me. . . .*
> > *you are familiar with all my ways.*
> *Before a word is on my tongue*
> > *you know it completely, O L*ORD.
> *Such knowledge*
> > *is too wonderful for me.*
> *All the days ordained for me*
> > *were written in your book*
> > > *before one of them came to be.*
> *How precious to me*
> > *are your thoughts, O God!*
> > > *—Psalm 139:1,3,4,6,16,17*

*Teach me, O L*ORD*, to follow your decrees;*
> *Then I will keep them to the end.*
Direct me in the path of your commands,
> *for there I find delight.*
Turn my heart toward your statutes
> *and not toward selfish gain.*
Turn my eyes away from worthless things;
> *renew my life according to your word.*
> > *—Psalm 119:33,35-37*

A FRESH START

Could it be that
    you are wondering
        if you are fitting into
        God's plan for your life?

You were born into a situation
    over which you had no control.
Decisions you have made—
    and those others have made
        for you—
    along with many other circumstances
        have determined
            who and what you are *now*.

As you look back
    over the course of events
        in your life,
    can you recognize that God
        has had his hand in it?

When making decisions,
    do you pause for a moment
    and ask the Lord to help you
        make the *right* one?

With the first day
    of the rest of your life
        ahead of you, *now* what?
Will those be days, hours, and moments
    of significant achievement
        in the light of
            eternal values?
They can be!

Job, speaking to the LORD,
> *"I know that you can do
> all things;
> no plan of yours
> can be thwarted."*
> —Job 42:1,2

Teach me your way, O LORD;
> *lead me in a straight path.*
> —Psalm 27:11

*The eyes of the Lord
> are on the righteous
> and his ears are attentive
> to their prayer.*
> —1 Peter 3:12

The LORD *blessed
> the latter part of
> Job's life
> more than the first.*
> —Job 42:12

TAKING INVENTORY

As you think back about
    your way of life
        throughout the years,
do you wonder whether
    you will someday hear
God say to you,
    "Well done,
        good and faithful servant!"?

Perhaps this would be a good time
    to take inventory—
to make an appraisal of
    your talents and skills.

List your qualifications—
    the things you like to do
        and those you do best.

Ask the Lord to open your eyes
    to the possibilities
        of using your talents
           to glorify him.

By putting your special abilities
    to work for the Lord,
    you will *receive* his blessing,
    and you will *become*
        a blessing to others.

Surely, retirement years
    are not the time
        to lay aside
    your gifts and talents,
but rather to use them
    in new, creative, and
        fulfilling ways.

*We have different gifts,
   according to the grace
      given us.
If a man's gift is . . .
   teaching, let him teach;
if it is encouraging,
   let him encourage;
if it is contributing
   to the needs of others,
   let him give generously; . . .
if it is showing mercy,
   let him do it cheerfully.*
         —Romans 12:6-8

*Jesus told his disciples:
   "The Son of Man [Jesus]
      is going to come
      in his Father's glory
         with his angels,
   and then he will reward
      each person
      according to what
         he has done."*
         —Matthew 16:27

*Fire will test the quality
   of each man's work.
If what he has built survives,
   he will receive his reward.*
         —1 Corinthians 3:13,14

*I will instruct you
 and teach you
 in the way you should go;
I will counsel you
 and watch over you.
 —Psalm 32:8*

NO LONGER NEEDED?

As your children
        and grandchildren mature
      and your career comes to an end,
        you may feel that you are
          no longer needed.

Younger people,
    instead of having respect
        for your years of experience,
    may make you feel unwanted.

But the growth of your children
and the end
    of your active work life
do not mean
    you are no longer serving
        a useful purpose.

If you are a member of God's family,
    it is important
        that you continue
          in your dedication to Christ
            and his teaching.

Your peers
    and the younger generation
        need examples of holy living.

And the Church—
        the fellowship of believers—
asks for
    your prayers, your time,
    your service, your wisdom,
    and your presence.

You *are* needed!

Never be lacking in zeal,
*   but keep your spiritual fervor,*
*   serving the Lord.*
Be joyful in hope,
*   patient in affliction,*
*   faithful in prayer.*
Share with God's people
*   who are in need.*
*   Practice hospitality.*
*   —Romans 12:11-13*

As we have opportunity,
*   let us do good*
*   to all people.*
*   —Galatians 6:10*

Set your minds on things above,
*   not on earthly things.*
*   —Colossians 3:2*

Be joyful always;
*   pray continually;*
give thanks in all circumstances,
*   for this is God's will*
*   for you*
*   in Christ Jesus.*
*   —1 Thessalonians 5:16-18*

*God . . . richly provides us
    with everything
        for our enjoyment.*

*Be rich in good deeds . . .
    generous and willing to share.
        —1 Timothy 6:17,18*

*Children's children
are a crown
to the aged.
—Proverbs 17:6*

LONELY? . . . OR ALONE?

You can be lonely almost anywhere—
    in a nursing home,
    in a hospital,
    in a retirement center,
    even among your own family members.

You may long for friends,
    a companion . . .
        someone to talk to.

Or, you may be a "loner,"
    preferring to be independent—
        living and working alone,
        believing that your ten fingers
            are *your* best friends.
    Your enjoyment comes from some hobby,
        handicraft, or good books.

But, absorbed though you may be
        in such activities,
    at some time or other,
        you'll need a good friend.
And "There is a friend
    who sticks closer than a brother."

God's Son, Jesus Christ,
    wants you to know him
        as *your* Friend.

In times of illness and suffering,
    or in times when you simply
        have no companions,
    He is there. Call on Him!

What a friend we have in Jesus!

WHAT A FRIEND

What a Friend we have in Jesus,
    All our sins and griefs to bear!
What a privilege to carry
    Everything to God in prayer!
O what peace we often forfeit,
    O what needless pain we bear,
All because we do not carry
    Ev'rything to God in prayer!

Have we trials and temptations?
    Is there trouble anywhere?
We should never be discouraged,
    Take it to the Lord in prayer.
Can we find a friend so faithful
    Who will all our sorrows share?
Jesus knows our every weakness,
    Take it to the Lord in prayer.

Are we weak and heavy-laden,
    Cumbered with a load of care?—
Precious Savior, still our refuge,—
    Take it to the Lord in prayer.
Do thy friends despise, forsake thee?
    Take it to the Lord in prayer;
In His arms He'll take and shield thee,
    Thou wilt find a solace there.

          —Joseph Scriven

HAPPINESS IS . . .

There are so many things
   in life that can bring
      gladness to your heart . . .

There's the joy of music
   that comes from playing—
      or simply listening to—
an old familiar tune.

Or those moments of exultation
   that come as you watch
      a glorious sunset
      or brilliant rainbow.

Perhaps it was your child's
   very first words or steps
      that made a moment special.

As you look back upon
   those times of your life
      when you were surprised by joy,
you realize how simple
   the circumstances often were
      that brought on
         those feelings of happiness.

Let your joy have its source
   in doing things for others.
Use every opportunity to do
   a kind deed for someone.
Give generously of yourself,
   and those moments of joy
      will multiply for you.

May the God of hope
    fill you
        with all joy and peace
        as you trust in him,
so that you may overflow
    with hope
    by the power
        of the Holy Spirit.
        —Romans 15:13

You [O God] have made known to me
    the path of life;
you will fill me
    with joy in your presence.
        —Psalm 16:11

HEALTH

Perhaps the greatest problem
   we face as we grow older
      is the decline of our health—
         the loss of youthful vigor,
         the inability to be as active
           as we once were.

God has not promised his children
   that they will never be ill
      or lose the strength of their youth.

Great men and women of God
   have suffered much physical pain.
Yet the person who is dedicated to God
   knows that his life and health
      are in God's hands.

You do well to pray for relief
   from your physical problems—
      and even more than that—
         to be *preserved from* such ills.

But if declining health does come,
   you will still be able
      to praise God
         and trust in his love.

You know that he cares for you
   and will not forsake you
      no matter what trials
         you may have.

And though your health may be waning,
   God had promised his children
      a future life without pain, tears,
      or death—a glorious, everlasting life!

*Dear Friend,
I pray that you may enjoy good health
and that all may go well with you,
even as your soul,
is getting along well.
—3 John 2*

*Answer me when I call to you,
O my righteous God.
Give me relief from my distress;
be merciful to me
and hear my prayer.
—Psalm 4:1*

*The Lord said to the Apostle Paul,
"My grace is sufficient for you,
for my power is made perfect
in weakness."
Therefore I will boast
all the more gladly
about my weaknesses,
so that Christ's power
may rest on me. . . .
For when I am weak,
then I am strong.
—2 Corinthians 12:9,10*

*God has promised that he
"will wipe every tear
from their eyes.
There will be no more death
or mourning or crying or pain,
for the old order of things
has passed away."
—Revelation 21:4*

COPING WITH CHANGE

Sometimes it seems that there is
 only one constant thing—
CHANGE!
 Change in work habits,
 Change in family relations,
 Change in living arrangements,
 Change in health and appearance,
 Change in attitude.

But changing is part of aging!

Sometimes the changes are dizzying—
 almost too much to cope with.
You begin to wonder if anything is stable
 or if anyone cares about
  what the changes do to you.

To be sure, your Heavenly Father cares.
 He cares when changes in health
  affect you and those around you.
 He cares when you have to adjust
  to new living arrangements.
 He cares when you hurt
  because those you love
   are too busy with their own lives
   to be attentive to your needs.

The Scriptures encourage you
 to take your burdens to the Lord
 because he is concerned about you.

There is no anxiety you need face alone,
 for the Heavenly Father
  truly cares for you.

Jesus said:
"Do not let your hearts
be troubled.
Trust in God;
trust also in me.

"I have told you these things,
so that in me
you may have peace.
In this world
you will have trouble.
But take heart!
I have overcome the world."
—John 14:1, 16:33

The Apostle Paul said:
"I have learned
to be content
whatever the circumstances. . . .
I have learned the secret
of being content
in any and every situation, . . .
I can do everything
through Him
who gives me strength."
—Philippians 4:11–13

Cast all your anxiety
on him [God]
because he cares for you.
—1 Peter 5:7

PEACE FOR ANXIETY

Did worry ever make
 a bad situation better?
Of course not!
Yet, how good we are at worrying,
 and how easy it is
  when there seems to be
  so much to fret about.

You may ask:
 Will my health hold up?
 Will I have to leave my home?
 Will I lose touch with my family?
 Will I have enough money?
 Will I become bored with retirement?

Such questions are bound to arise,
 but there is no need to let them
  take possession of your mind.

Endless dialogue with yourself
 will not change the situation.
But there is a way to replace
 those troubling thoughts
  with tranquil ones!

The loving, Heavenly Father,
 again and again, invites you
  to simply trust him
  with your anxieties.

Commit your cares and concerns
 to the Lord.
His peace will keep your thoughts
 quiet and at rest
  as you trust him.

He promised!

Jesus said,
> *"I tell you, do not worry*
> > *about your life,*
> > > *what you will eat or drink;*
> > *or about your body,*
> > > *what you will wear.*
> *Is not life more important*
> > *than food,*
> *and the body more important*
> > *than clothes?*
>
> *"Look at the birds of the air;*
> > *they do not sow or reap*
> > > *or store away in barns,*
> > *and yet your heavenly Father*
> > > *feeds them.*
> *Are you not much more valuable*
> > *than they?*
> *Who of you by worrying*
> > *can add a single hour*
> > > *to his life?"*
> > > > *—Matthew 6:25-27*

Do not be anxious about anything,
> *but in everything,*
> > *by prayer and petition,*
> > > *with thanksgiving,*
> *present your requests to God.*
And the peace of God,
> *which transcends*
> *all understanding,*
> *will guard your hearts*
> *and your minds*
> *in Christ Jesus.*
> > > *—Philippians 4:6,7*

JOYOUS TIMES

Time, it seems, becomes more precious
    as we grow older!

If you love life,
    you won't squander your time.

Those "golden age" moments
    can be used so profitably—
        enjoying your grandchildren,
            telling them stories,
            planning surprises for them,
            praying with them and for them,
            teaching *them* to pray.

You have no grandchildren?
    "Adopt" one!
Some children have no grandparents!

Now is the time to enjoy
    the fruit of your life's labors.

As your daily work routines
    and family commitments
        become less demanding,
take time to realize your dreams—
    visiting a dear friend,
    painting a picture,
    handcrafting a gift,
    reading or writing,
    gardening—and sharing
        from your abundant yield.
If cooking is your talent,
    treat your neighbor to a special dish.

Be a blessing, and showers of blessings
    will attend your way!

*Since my youth, O God,
    you have taught me,
and to this day I declare
    your marvelous deeds.
Even when I am old and gray,
    do not forsake me, O God,
        till I declare your power
        to the next generation.
            —Psalm 71:17,18*

A THANKFUL HEART

You have been blessed
    with long life,
  and, as you look back
    upon your years,
  pleasant memories
    flow through your mind.

It has been said that
  "Age is a quality of mind."

One of the sources of happiness
  is to have as many
    pleasant thoughts
    as possible. . . .

Let those thoughts of your heart
  flow out in your speech.

A soul-refreshing practice
  is to acknowledge,
    with sincere gladness,
  the benefits and mercies
    of the Lord's goodness
    to you.

It's quite true, as Shakespeare wrote,
  "The web of our life
    is of mingled yarn,
      good and ill together."
But focusing in on the
    cheery side of life
  sweetens the soul
    and is good for your health.

Make yours an attitude of gratitude!

Jesus said,
"Out of the overflow
of the heart
the mouth speaks.
The good man brings good things
out of the good
stored up in him."
—Matthew 12:34,35

Whatever is true,
whatever is noble,
whatever is right,
whatever is pure,
whatever is lovely,
whatever is admirable—
if anything is excellent
or praiseworthy—
think about such things.
—Philippians 4:8

It is good to praise the LORD
and make music to your name,
O Most High,
to proclaim your love
in the morning
and your faithfulness
at night.
—Psalm 92:1,2

Pleasant words are a honeycomb,
sweet to the soul and
healing to the bones.
—Proverbs 16:24

TIME TO PRAY

The busy pace of life
    during youth and middle age
        often leaves little time
           for prayer.
As we grow older, however,
    there often is more freedom,
        more hours open,
           fewer commitments than before.

Do *you* have more free time now?

Use that time to pray!

Again and again, the Scriptures
    encourage us to seek after God,
        to come into his presence . . .
           to talk with him.

Again and again, the Scriptures
    tell us how God rewards those
        who diligently seek him.

What a precious privilege it is
    to enter the royal throne room
        and speak with the
           King of kings and Lord of lords.

You will do well
    to set aside a special time each day
        to meet and talk with the Lord.

No power on earth can compare
    with the prayer of the person
        who keeps in close touch with God.

Learn how to pray . . . effectively!

The Lord Almighty said,
"Call upon me
and come and pray to me,
and I will listen to you.
You will seek me and find me
when you seek me
with all your heart.

"Call to me
and I will answer you
and tell you great and
unsearchable things
you do not know."
—Jeremiah 29:12,13; 33:3

Let us then approach
the throne of grace
with confidence,
so that we may receive mercy
and find grace to help us
in our time of need.
—Hebrews 4:16

The prayer of a righteous man
is powerful and effective.
—James 5:16

Seek the LORD
 while he may be found;
call on him
 while he is near.
 —Isaiah 55:6

I love the LORD,
 for he heard my voice; . . .
Because he turned his ear to me,
 I will call on him
  as long as I live.
    —Psalm 116:1,2

YOUR FUTURE

There comes a moment in everyone's life
>   when time merges into eternity—
>   when we pass through death's door
>   into a different kind of existence . . .
>   for better or for worse—eternally!

Our future depends upon
>   our relationship with God
>   while we are here on earth.

Jesus, God's Son, came to this earth,
>   from his heavenly home,
>   to restore the relationship
>   of sinful man to his Maker
>   by dying in our place.
>   He talked about that home
>   and told us how to get there.

The spiritual birth
>   that brings you into God's family,
>   not only prepares you
>   for a glorious eternal life
>   but enhances your life
>   here on earth as well.

God's forgiveness of your sins
>   brings peace to your soul
>   and hope for your future!

Your relationship with your Creator
>   is restored,
>   and life takes on new meaning.

So . . . what, on earth,
>   are you doing about Heaven?

*The LORD is my shepherd,
    I shall lack nothing.
He makes me lie down
        in green pastures,
    he leads me beside quiet waters,
        he restores my soul.
He guides me
    in paths of righteousness
        for his name's sake.
Even though I walk
    through the valley
        of the shadow of death,
I will fear no evil,
    for you are with me;
        your rod and your staff,
            they comfort me.
You prepare a table before me
    in the presence of my enemies.
You anoint my head with oil;
    my cup overflows.
Surely goodness and love
    will follow me
        all the days of my life,
    and I will dwell
        in the house of the LORD
            forever.
            —Psalm 23*

A GLORIOUS FUTURE

Your destination . . .
>   The place you hope
>   to reach.

Paradise?
That's what Jesus called
>   *his* destination
>   when he was about
>   to return to Heaven.
Just before he died,
>   he promised the thief
>   on the cross next to his,
"Today you will be with me
>   in Paradise!"

The evening before,
>   Jesus had told his disciples
>   that he was going
>   to his Father's house
>   "to prepare a place
>   for them" . . .
>   and for all who receive him
>   as their Savior.

And what a place that is! . . .
>   A place without suffering,
>   A place without grief,
>   A place without pain,
>   A place without sin.
>   A place, the grandeur of which
>   our minds cannot imagine.

What a glorious future
>   is ahead for those
>   who love the Lord!

Precious
 in the sight of the LORD
 is the death of his saints.
  —Psalm 116:15

Jesus said:
 "In my Father's house
  are many rooms; . . .
 I am going there to prepare
  a place for you."
  —John 14:2

"No eye has seen,
 no ear has heard,
  no mind has conceived
 what God has prepared
  for those who love him."
  —1 Corinthians 2:9

Nothing impure
 will ever enter it
  [the Holy City out of Heaven] . . .
but only those whose names
 are written in the
  Lamb's book of life.
   —Revelation 21:27

ABUNDANT LIFE

How very fragile
   physical life really is,
   but how unending
      your spiritual life will be.

How important, then,
   to live each day
   as though it were your last.

One of the most satisfying
   experiences you can have
      is a spiritual one—
   introducing others
      to the Lord Jesus Christ . . .
   explaining to them
      God's plan of salvation.

There is no joy that compares
   with assisting someone else
      to commit his life
         to the Lord—
      pointing the way
      to eternal life.

If you yourself
   do not know the Lord Jesus
      as your personal Savior,
   why not place your trust in him
      right now
      by praying the prayer
         on page 46.

Jesus said,
> *"I have come*
>> *that they may have life,*
>> *and have it to the full."*
>>> *—John 10:10*

Do not boast about tomorrow,
> *for you do not know*
>> *what a day*
>>> *may bring forth.*
>>>> *—Proverbs 27:1*

Multitudes who sleep
> *in the dust of the earth*
> *will awake:*
> *some to everlasting life,*
> *others to shame and*
>> *everlasting contempt.*

Those who are wise
> *will shine*
>> *like the brightness*
>>> *of the heavens,*

and those who lead many
> *to righteousness,*
>> *like the stars*
>> *for ever and ever.*
>>> *—Daniel 12:2,3*

PRAYER

Dear God,

I believe that your Son, Jesus,
    died on a cross
        to pay the penalty
        for my sin
    and that he rose again
        that I might have
            eternal life.

Please forgive all my sin
    and cleanse my life
        so that I may fit into
        Your plan for my life
            from this day on.

I want You to be
    my Lord and Master
        the rest of my days
            here on earth
    so that my life
        will be pleasing to You.

Thank-you, Lord, for providing
    eternal life for me!

I pray this in Jesus' name.
        Amen.

Jesus said,
"I tell you the truth,
unless a man is
born again,
he cannot see
the kingdom of God.

"Flesh gives birth to flesh,
but the [Holy] Spirit
gives birth to spirit.

"For God so loved the world
that he gave
his one and only Son,
that whoever believes in him
shall not perish
but have eternal life."
—John 3:3,6,16

If you confess with your mouth,
"Jesus is Lord,"
and believe in your heart
that God raised him
from the dead,
you will be saved.
For it is with your heart
that you believe
and are justified,
and it is with your mouth
that you confess
and are saved.
—Romans 10:9,10

This booklet has been given to you by:

PROJECT PHILIP
P.O. BOX 1423
ESCONDIDO, CA 92033

If you would like to have further help
in learning how to live
and walk with God,
please write us or call us.

We will be happy to help you!